WORLD WINDOWS

Push and Pull

HEINLE
CENGAGE Learning

YSG A YBM COMPANY Young & Son Global, Inc.

How do you open a door?

Contents

Vocabulary

move

push

pull

away from
closer to
things

How to Move Things

How do you move things?
You can move things by pushing or pulling them.

Pushing and pulling makes things move in different ways.

Push

Pushing makes things move away from you.

When you push a door, the door moves away from you.

When you push a cart, the cart moves away from you.

When you push a stroller, the stroller moves away from you.

Pull

Pulling makes things move closer to you.
When you pull a wagon, the wagon moves closer to you.

When you pull a sled, the sled moves closer to you.

When you pull a rope, the other person moves closer to you.

Summary

How do you move these things?

Song

If You Want to Move a Sled

If you want to move a sled, pull the sled.
If you want to move a cart, push the cart.
If you want to move something,
You can push or pull.
Pushing and pulling makes something move.

If you want to move a sled, pull the sled.
If you want to move a cart, push the cart.
If you want to move something,
You can push or pull.
Pushing and pulling makes something move.

Index